Hanse and Gretel

Written by Malachy Doyle
Illustrated by Tim Archbold

 Collins

"There is no food," said the woodman.
"How will we eat?"
"Take Hansel and Gretel for a walk in
the Brown Wood," said his wife, "and
leave them."

"No!" said the woodman. "I cannot!"
"You must, or we will all die!" cried his wife.

So the woodman took Hansel and Gretel into the Brown Wood.

He gave the boy and girl some cake to eat. But Hansel put it in his pocket and dropped little bits all along the way.

The woodman left Hansel and Gretel deep
inside the dark, dark wood.
He walked away and did not look back.

"Now we are all alone! How will we get home?"
Gretel sobbed.

"Do not cry," said Hansel. "We will see the cake
I dropped in the dirt, and it will lead us home."

But the birds came flying down from the sky.
They saw the cake all along the way, and
they ate it all up. Caw! Caw!

Hansel and Gretel were lost.
They walked on and on till they were
very hungry.

Then they saw a small house.
A sweet little granny was outside.
"Come in and eat," she said.

But when they got in she locked the gate.
"I will make you fat!" she hissed.
"I will toss you in this cauldron and cook
you and eat you!"

But Gretel grabbed her hair and
threw her in the cauldron!
They unlocked the gate and
ran away as fast as they could.

"We will show you the way home," said
the birds. Caw! Caw!

When they got home, the woodman ran out
to greet them.
"I'm so glad to have you back!" he cried.
Hansel and Gretel were happy then, and
the woodman did not send them away again.

A story map

:paw: Ideas for reading :paw:

Learning objectives: Blend phonemes for reading; Use phonological knowledge to work out, predict and check the meanings of unfamiliar words; Read on sight high frequency words.

Curriculum links: Citizenship: Children's rights

Focus phonemes: oy (boy), ir (birds, girl, dirt), au (cauldron), al (walk), aw (caw, saw), air (hair)

Fast words: were, very, could, put

Word count: 297

Getting started

- Write the words that feature the focus phonemes *oy, ir, au, al, aw* and *air* on a small whiteboard and ask the group to fast-read them, blending aloud if they need to.

- Give the children a brief introduction to the main characters in this story, writing their names on the whiteboard. Explain that the family is very poor. Ask the children to guess what the woodman and his wife might do to save them from starvation.

- Write *woodman, pocket, sobbed, toss, grabbed, cauldron* and *greet* on the whiteboard to double-check that the children understand the meanings of the words.

- Hand out the books and read pp2–3 together. Ask the children how they feel about the wife's idea.

Reading and responding

- Ask the children to continue reading the book independently.

- Listen in as the children read pp4–5. Before reading on, ask the children to talk about Hansels' idea. Ask: *What was he planning to do? Will his plan work?*

- Move around the class as the children read on, listening in to check that the children are blending unfamiliar words correctly. When reading p7, ask: *How do you know how to read the birds' sounds?*